GIANNI A. SARCONE
MARIE-JO WAEBER

AMAZING
OPTICAL
ILLUSIONS

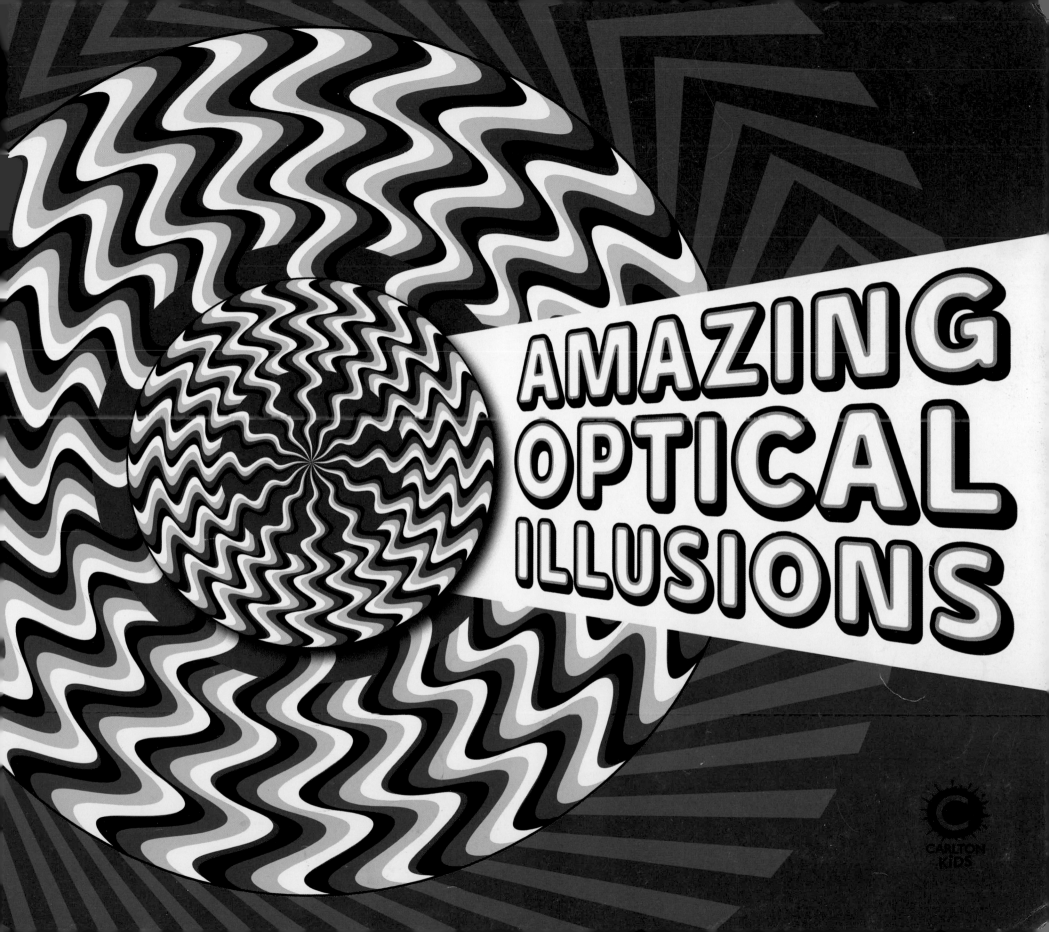

AMAZING OPTICAL ILLUSIONS

AMAZING OPTICAL ILLUSIONS

GIANNI A. SARCONE
AND MARIE-JO WAEBER

WARNING!

YOU ARE NOW ENTERING

THE DIZZY ZONE

HOLD ON TIGHT FOR THE NEXT FEW PAGES.

Here are illusions to scramble your eyeballs, boggle your brain and turn your knees to jelly...

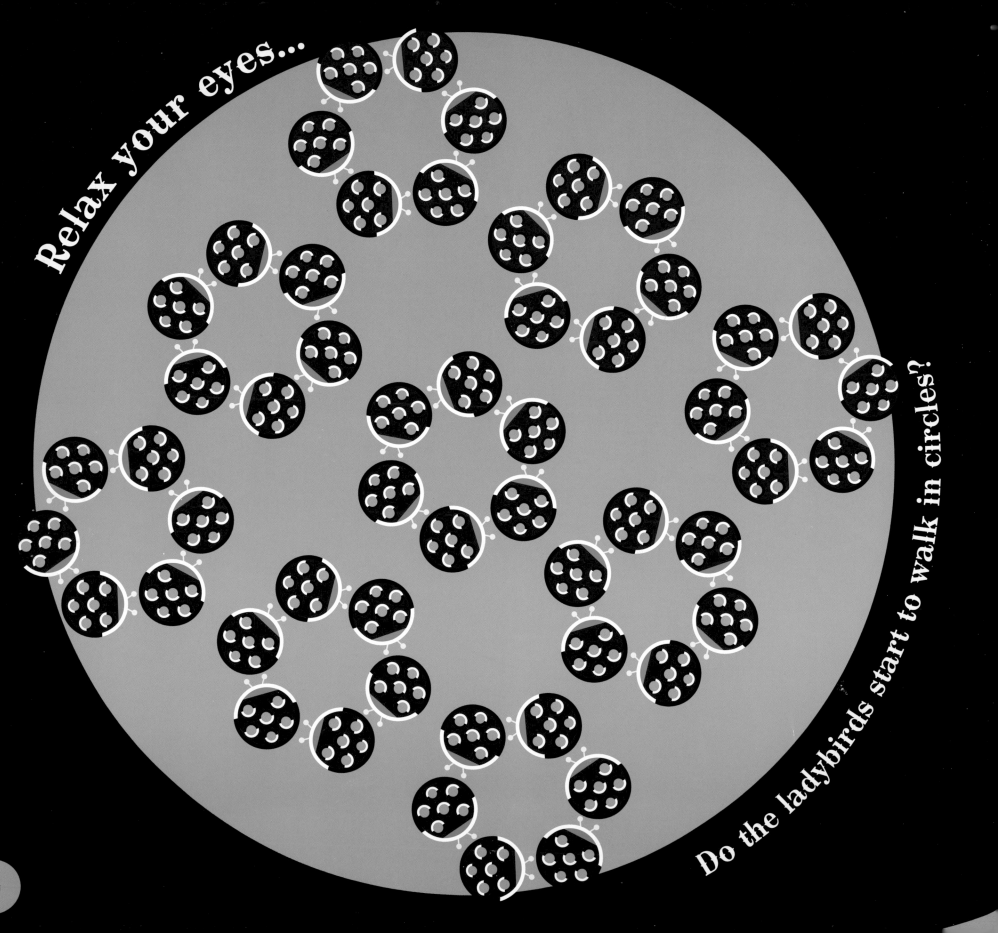

Relax your eyes...

Do the ladybirds start to walk in circles?

WATCH

**AS THIS
NEST OF
VIPERS
BEGINS TO UNCOIL...**

Each 'snake' is a set of smaller and smaller rings, with their colours not quite lined up. But your brain likes to keep things simple and orderly. So it tries to make the patterns line up by 'twisting' the rings in your mind, making them appear to turn.

9

MOVE YOUR EYES AROUND THIS GRID AND WATCH AS
THE DOTS CHANGE FROM GREY TO WHITE TO GREY AGAIN...

Looking straight at a spot shows it's really white. But when you look slightly to the side, your brain saves time and effort by guessing that the grey lines continue through the spot, and so it looks grey too.

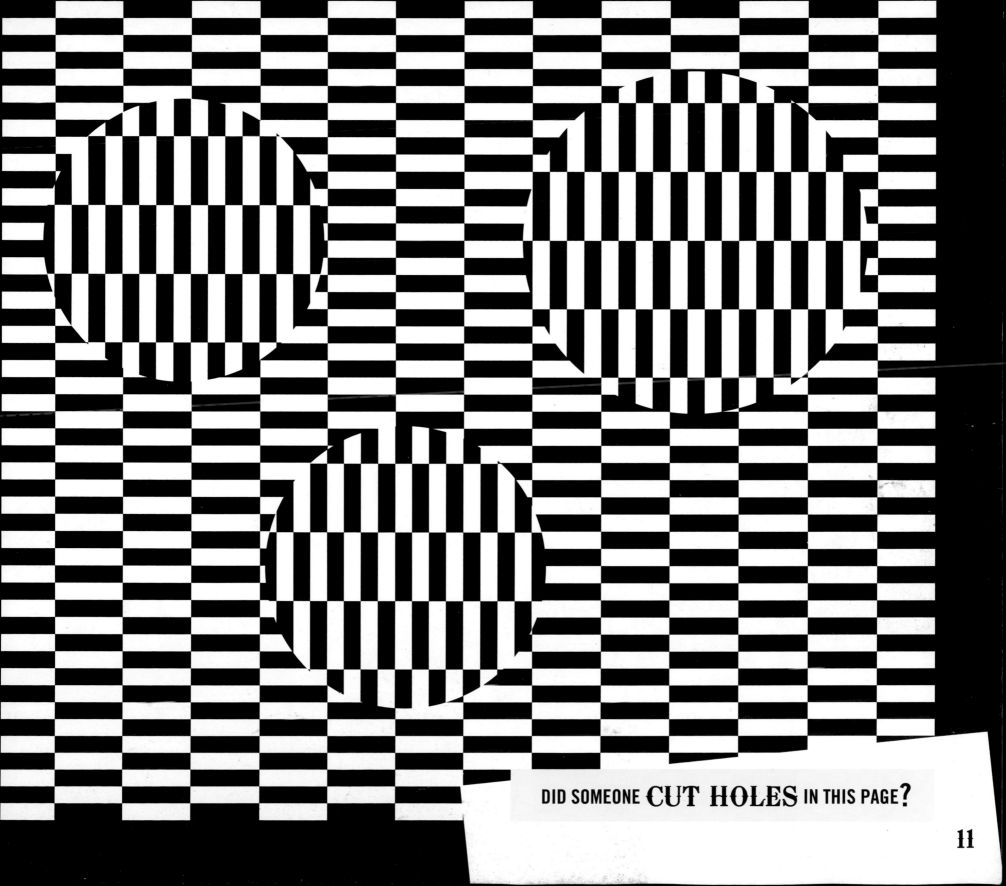

DID SOMEONE CUT HOLES IN THIS PAGE?

11

HEY!

Who stretched the book?

On a real rounded object, like a ball, any parts of a surface pattern gradually look thinner as they curve away. This effect, where more distant things look smaller, is called perspective, and the flat pattern here copies it.

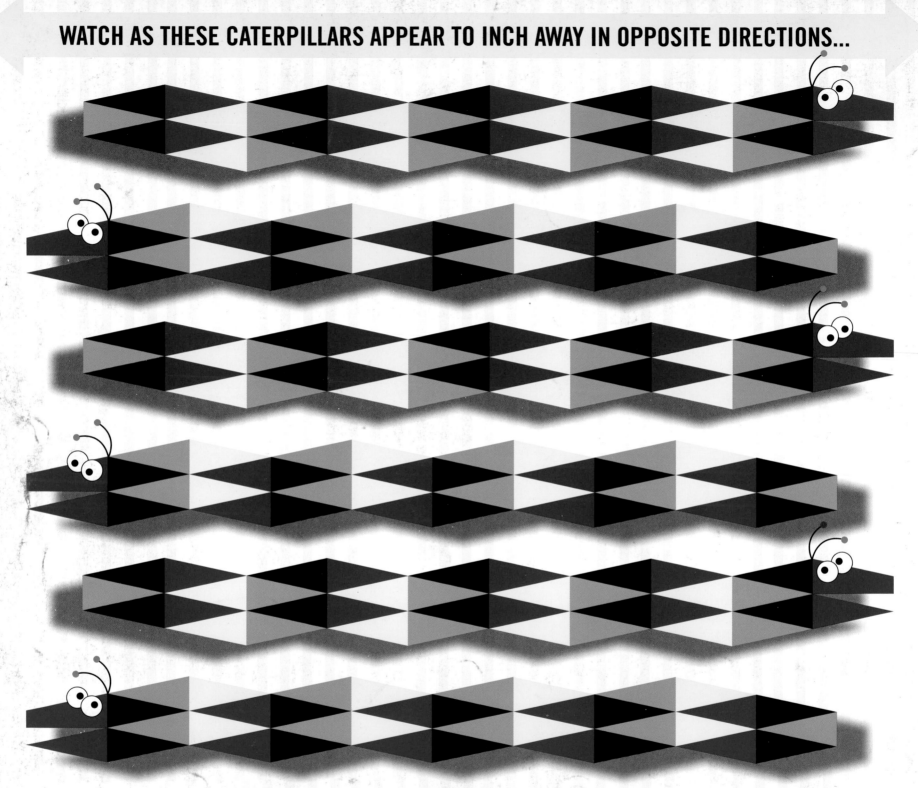

The caterpillars are not quite lined up, one below the other. But your brain wants them to be, to look neat. So it makes the caterpillars 'creep' into line. The effect is increased by the shadows which always point away from the caterpillars' heads.

FEELING DIZZY YET?

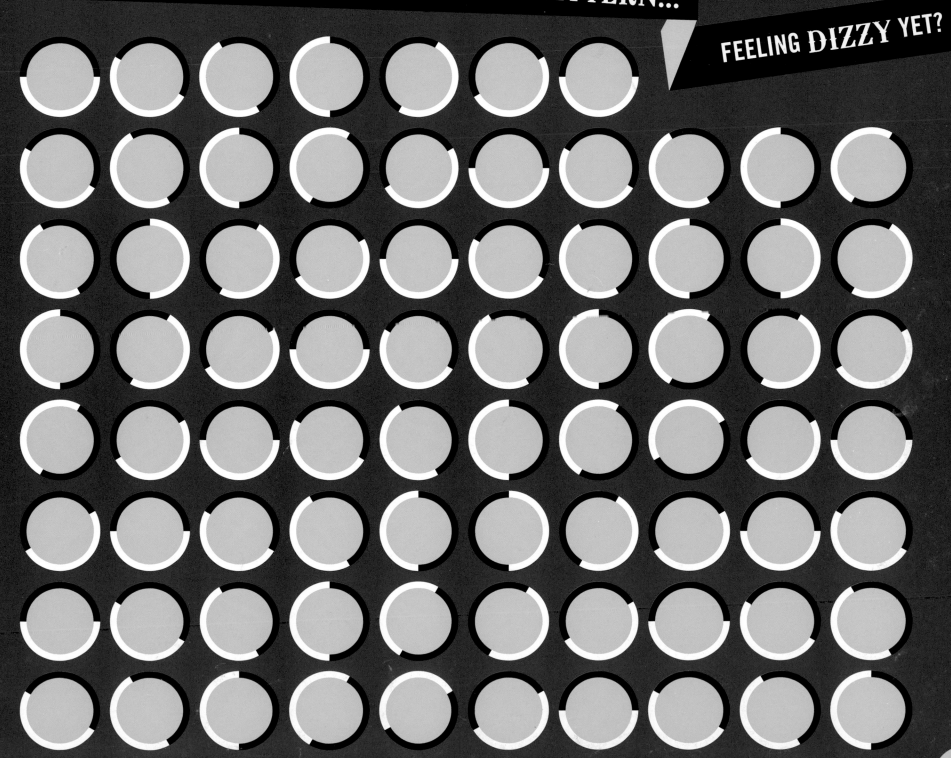

15

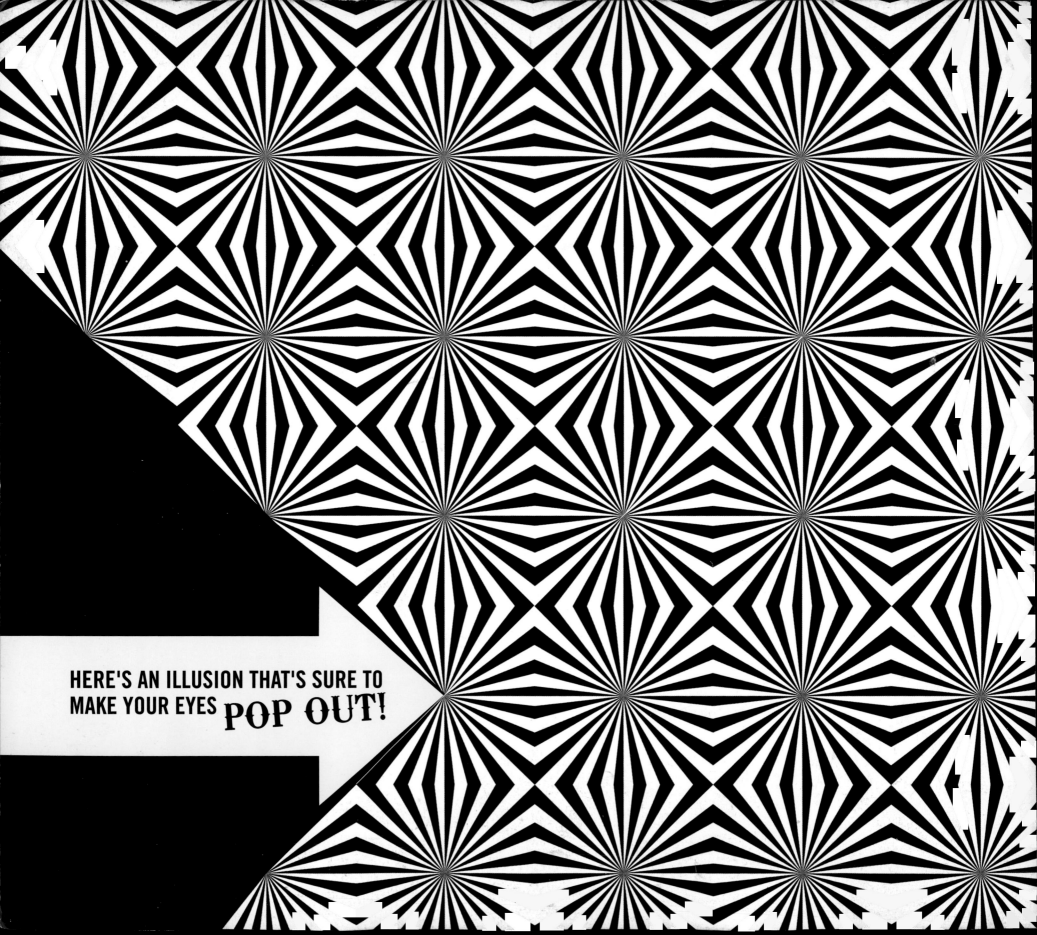

HERE'S AN ILLUSION THAT'S SURE TO
MAKE YOUR EYES POP OUT!

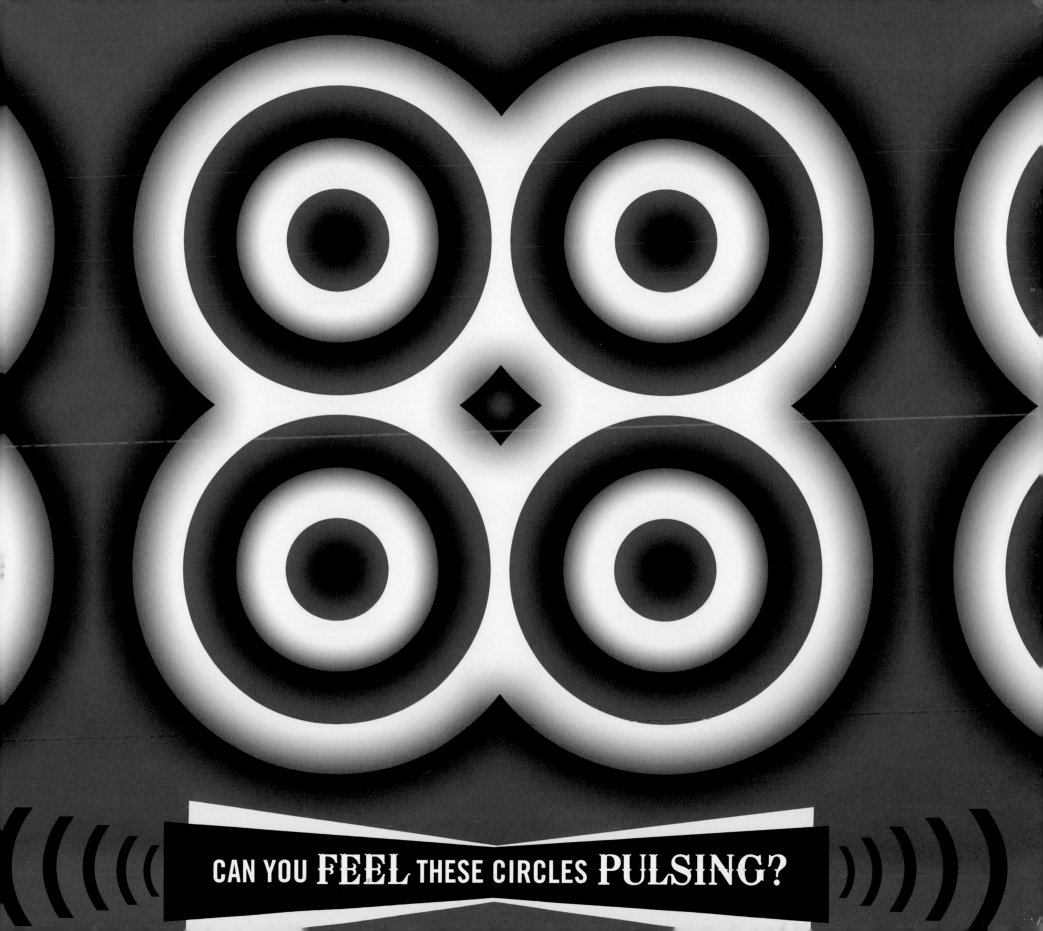

CAN YOU **FEEL** THESE CIRCLES **PULSING?**

LOOK

... and look again!

NOTHING IS QUITE AS IT SEEMS IN THE FOLLOWING PAGES.

Look out for impossible objects,
hidden secrets and doorways to incredible worlds...

Are you looking at a painting of a view from a window, or the actual view? Artist René Magritte (1898-1967) often painted common objects and familiar scenes, but put them together in an unusual way.

Plenty to drink
but not a glass in sight **?**

OR

just rows of glasses
with nothing to fill them **?**

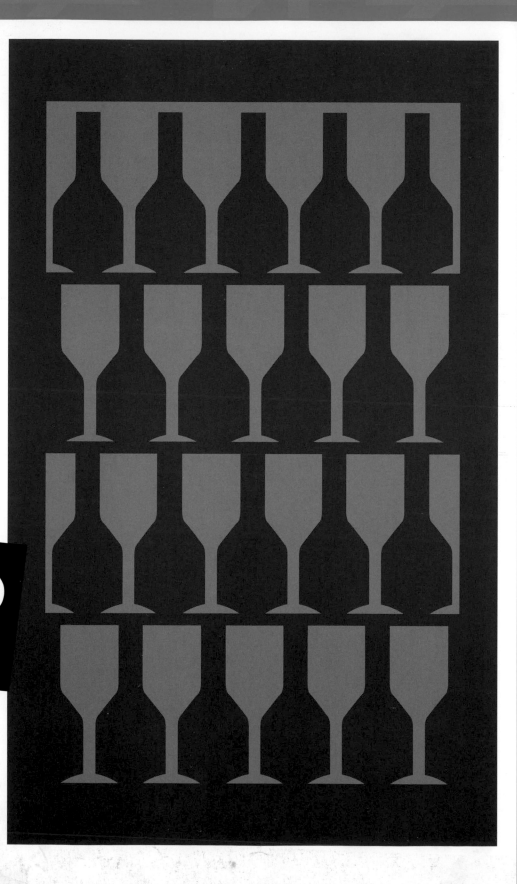

20

What a beautiful display of fruit!

BUT CAN YOU FIND TWO HUNGRY PEOPLE READY TO START EATING?

The brain quickly sees the bright, colourful fruit. Then it notices two white faces created by the outline of the fruit. So it 'flips' between the two views. This is called a figure-ground illusion, where the fruit is the figure (the main object) and the faces are the ground (background).

IS THIS PERSON HAPPY OR SAD ?

We are so used to seeing faces, we 'force' these lines into facial features, depending on which way up they are. The happy forehead wrinkle becomes a glum mouth, the raised eyebrows turn into sad lines under the eyes, and so on.

Try turning the page upside down...

Try turning the page upside down...

DO YOU SEE LAZY ELEPHANTS?

OR LEAPING ELEPHANTS?

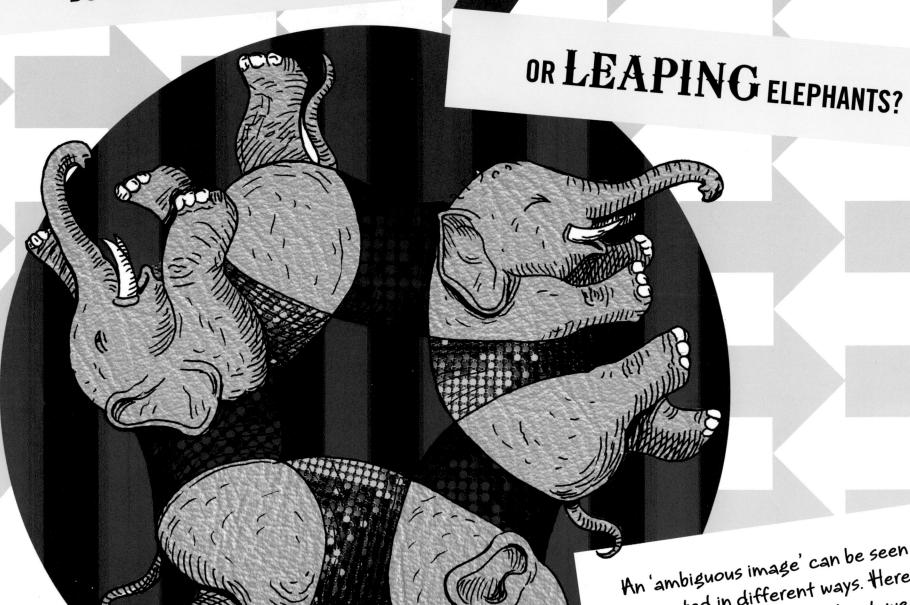

An 'ambiguous image' can be seen or interpreted in different ways. Here the back legs of a leaping elephant, wearing purple, are also the back legs of a lazy one, wearing green. Your brain cannot decide which set of elephants they belong to / to concentrate on.

THE CHESHIRE CAT SAYS THAT THE ARROWS WILL HELP ALICE TO FIND HER WAY.

BUT SHOULD SHE CHOOSE THE BLUE ONES OR THE WHITE ONES?

DOES THIS PERSON LOOK **STRANGE** OR **NORMAL** **PERFECTLY** **?**

(Now try turning the page upside down...)

26

WHAT DO YOU SEE ?

Billowing smoke from a fire on the hill...
or the flowing hair of a beautiful girl?

Tilt the page to read the secret message below...

NOW TILT THE PICTURE OPPOSITE AND LOOK IN THE DIRECTION OF THE ARROW TO FIND THE HIDDEN SKULL

In 1533, artist Hans Holbein stretched out an object so much, it became almost unrecognisable. But view it from a very low angle, and the true object is revealed! This effect, when objects viewed at an angle look shorter or squashed, is called 'foreshortening'.

This odd station entrance is really just a big drawing! The steps, railings, Alice, White Rabbit and other people have so much detail that they look three-dimensional. In fact they are drawn on the flat ground and the wall behind!

LOOK CLOSER...

COULD YOU REALLY WALK DOWN THESE STEPS?

LOOPY LINES
SILLY
& SIZES

THE NEXT ROUND OF ILLUSIONS IS ALL ABOUT SIZE, SHAPE AND DIRECTION.

If you suspect your eyes are playing tricks on you, grab this ruler and put the illusions to the test!

Is this really a spiral?

Trace one of the curved lines with your finger and decide for yourself!

Use your ruler to find out!

Here the short lines create a background that distorts the long parallel lines. Because the short lines are at an angle, they make one end of each long line seem closer than the other. The switching angle of the short lines makes the long lines appear to pull in opposite directions.

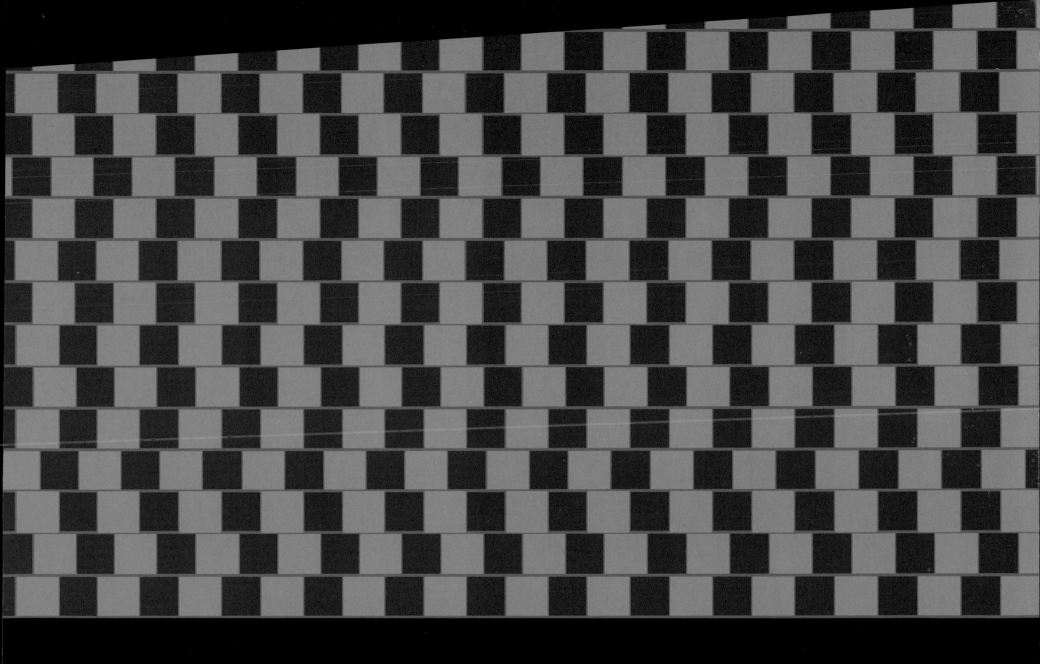

WHAT ABOUT THESE HORIZONTAL STRIPES?

Are they parallel or do they slope?

TWO PRETTY FLOWERS – BUT WHICH HAS THE **BIGGEST** ORANGE CENTRE?

When things are close together, we are good at comparing their sizes. Here the left flower's little petals make their centre look big, while the right flower's large petals make theirs seem smaller. But the two centres are far apart, so the brain does not realize that they are the same size.

Lines coming together show perspective and seem to go into the distance. The topmost banana is near to where the lines meet, so the brain thinks it's the furthest away. Yet because it looks the same size as the other bananas, we assume it's the biggest, too.

THIS MONKEY WANTS THE **BIGGEST** BANANA HE CAN FIND.

WHICH ONE SHOULD HE CHOOSE?

ARE THESE STARBURSTS ORANGE OR PURPLE?

Amazingly, they are all pink! The dots over each starburst make us see it in a colour that is more similar to, or assimilated into, its own. The differing colour of the background heightens the effect, known as colour assimilation and contrast.

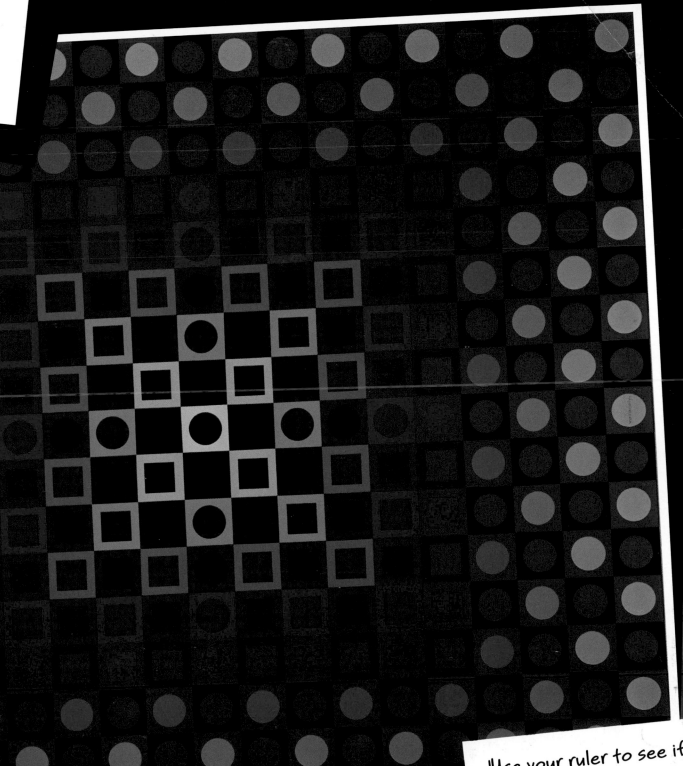

THIS CHECKERBOARD
PATTERN SEEMS EXTREMELY
WOBBLY AT THE CENTRE...

Use your ruler to see if
this is really the case.

THE GRAND TOUR OF CRAZY PLACES

ARE YOUR EYES SUFFICIENTLY SCRAMBLED?

If not, then join this tour of the most crazy places imaginable. Could they really exist?

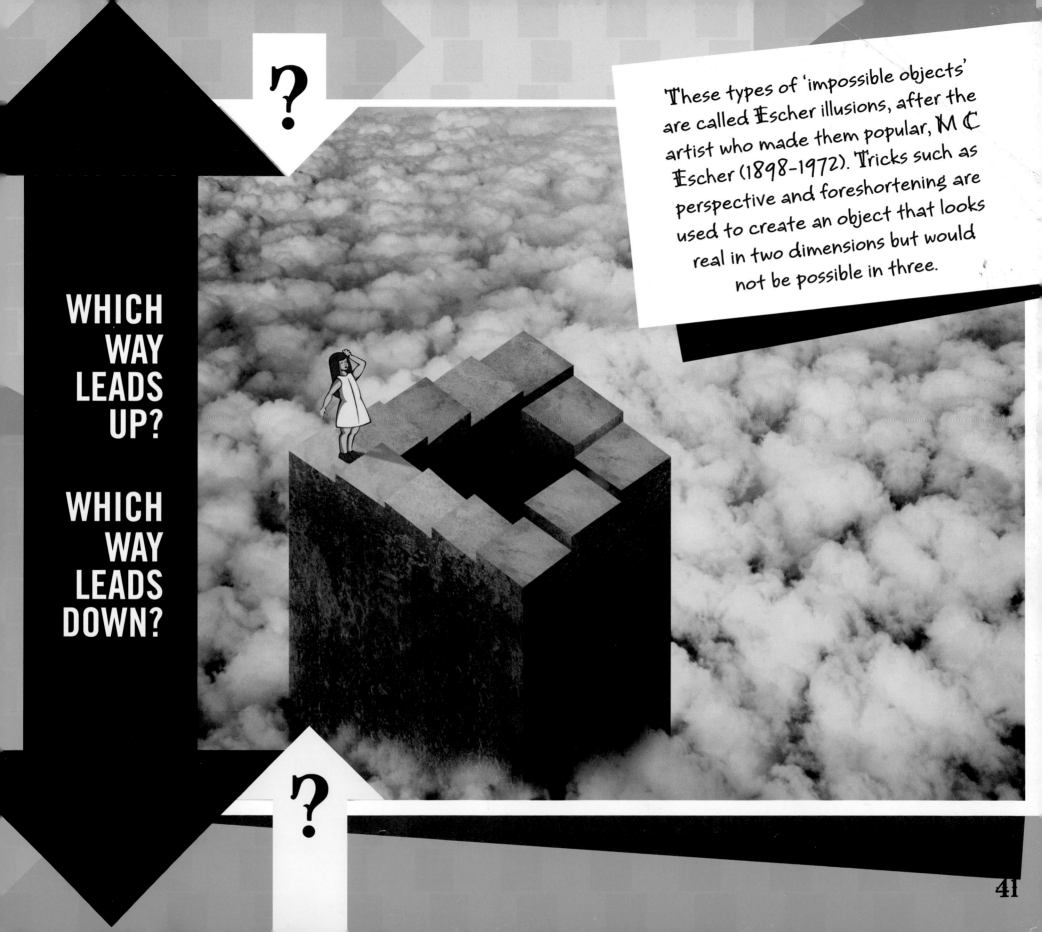

WHICH WAY LEADS UP?

WHICH WAY LEADS DOWN?

These types of 'impossible objects' are called Escher illusions, after the artist who made them popular, M C Escher (1898-1972). Tricks such as perspective and foreshortening are used to create an object that looks real in two dimensions but would not be possible in three.

LOONY LOOP

CURIOUS CUBE

SILLY CIRCLE

Could ANY of the exhibits in the **Museum of Wonders** really exist **?**

The truth is that none of these curious objects is possible. While they might look solid enough, the edges and surfaces combine in a way that simply couldn't exist. Try following an edge with your finger as if you were touching a real object – you'll soon find it to be **very strange indeed!**

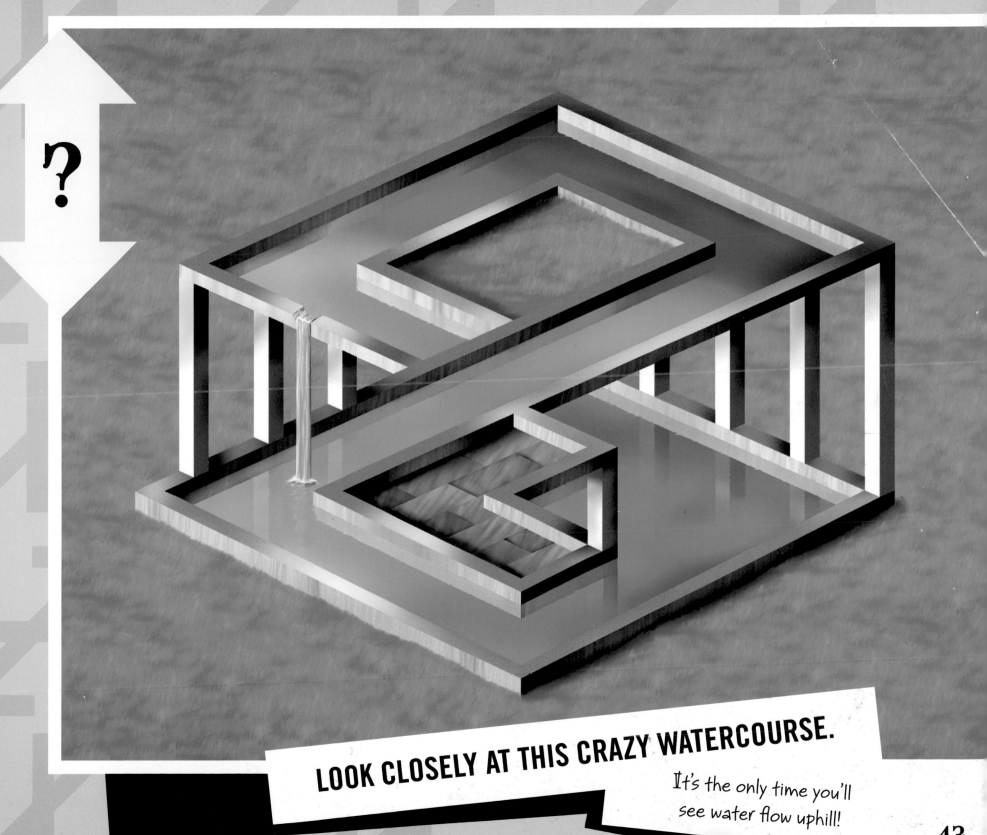

LOOK CLOSELY AT THIS CRAZY WATERCOURSE.

It's the only time you'll see water flow uphill!

CAN YOU DETECT SOMETHING STRANGE ABOUT THESE STEPS?

A CLUE: look closely at the grey bar halfway up the staircase...

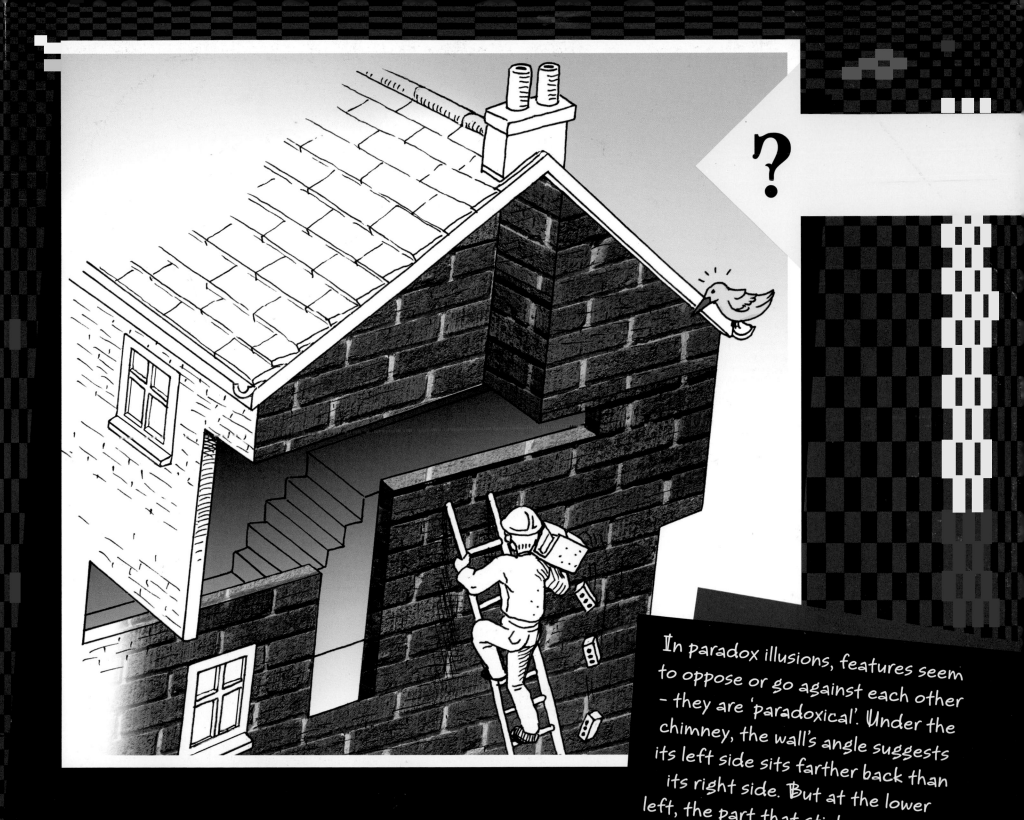

In paradox illusions, features seem to oppose or go against each other – they are 'paradoxical'. Under the chimney, the wall's angle suggests its left side sits farther back than its right side. But at the lower left, the part that sticks out makes the left side appear to be in front of the right.

How can three chimney openings have four bases? Look at the crane's load too! Long parallel lines are joined and shaded at one end to suggest one set of three-dimensional objects, but another set at the other end.

On the right, windows and steps give the impression of walls and flat floors. Follow the horizontal lines left, and the walls become floors, while the floors turn into walls. This illusion works best with a slight 'gap' in the middle of each level, with just horizontal lines and no other details.

ALL ABOUT
COLOURS

When we see a colour, we really see light being reflected from an object, which our brain "reads" as a particular colour. There's no colour in nature, because colours are actually all created in your brain!

Sometimes, as you'll see in the following pages, yo brain can be tricked and confuses colours and shad

DO YOU SEE SOME

GREEN DOTS?

Actually, they're not green but dark grey! You see green because of the colour of the background and the neighbouring shaded dots. Incredible, isn't it?

This football is covered with pentagonal and hexagonal panels.

Are panels A and B exactly the same SHADE?

Yes, they are! They look like different shades because they are surrounded by lighter and darker panels. Your brain is tricked by the contrast!

Cheshire Cat VANISH!

After approximately 20 seconds, the colours of the cat's face gradually disappear. Nothing is left behind but its grin!

To create the illusion of balance ...

stare at the fly in the right hand picture for 30 seconds, then look at the cow again. The photograph will look normal!

Can YOU see an orange EYE-SHAPE?

The dark orange glow of the outline is created by black lines on the yellow background. If you look closely you will see that there actually isn't any orange in this picture at all!

If you really concentrate on the middle of the picture, you might even get the eye to vanish!

Take a good look at this Greek painting. Are the arch shapes in the bottom and top row all the same **colour** and **shade**?

?

They are! This is hard to see because the human eye sees the outline of an object in relation to the colour of its background. Because the backgrounds are different colours it looks like the arches are, as well!

It looks like this cat has two green eyes, but really only one eye is green.

HOW DOES THAT WORK ?!

The right eye is grey, but seems tinted green because of the purple colour around it. When you look at the grey eye, your brain subtracts a bit of purple from the cat's face, which makes the eye look green. Cool, huh?

The colours of the rainbow in **figure A** are faded. To make them look stronger, stare at the white dot in **figure B** for 20 to 30 seconds, then shift your gaze back to **figure A**.

AMAZING, isn't it?

MATCH a pair of blue squares that have the same HUE and BRIGHTNESS.

Is it **A** and **C**, or **A** and **D**, or **B** and **C**, or maybe **B** and **D**?

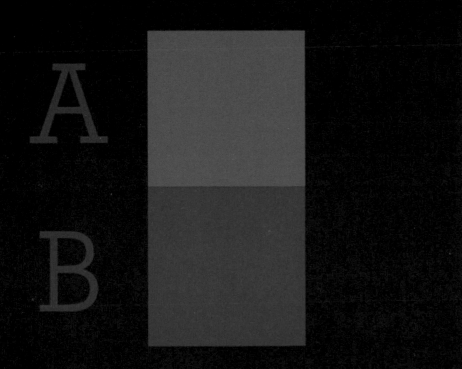

A

B

C

D

Answer: A is exactly the same shade as D, although the different backgrounds make A appear brighter than D.

Concentrate only on the square panels of the cubes

(the real one and its reflection).

WHICH PANELS SEEM **DARKER**?

In reality, the square panels of both cubes are identical! The illusion is created by the contrast between the backgrounds - in particular their brightness.

Then decide which ones have **YELLOW** inner circles, and which ones have **BLUE** inner circles.

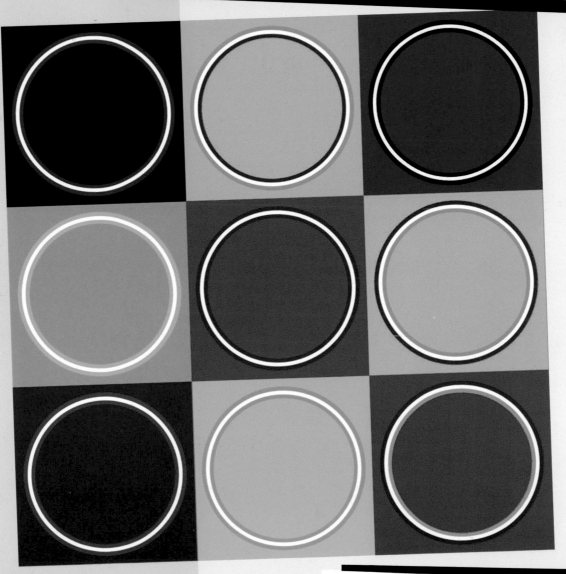

Ninety per cent of people answer that the rings in the first column have a blue inner circle, and those in the second and third columns have a yellow one. In fact, the middle colour inside all the rings is white!

WOW... IT MOVES!

Some repeated patterns can look like they are in motion. This is caused by very fast movements of your eyes that happen without you controlling them.

Be careful not to **stare** at this one for too long or you might become hypnotized!

Can you see the reddish portion of the pattern pulsating or throbbing? Try staring at it for a while and matching the "pulsations" of the picture with the beat of your heart!

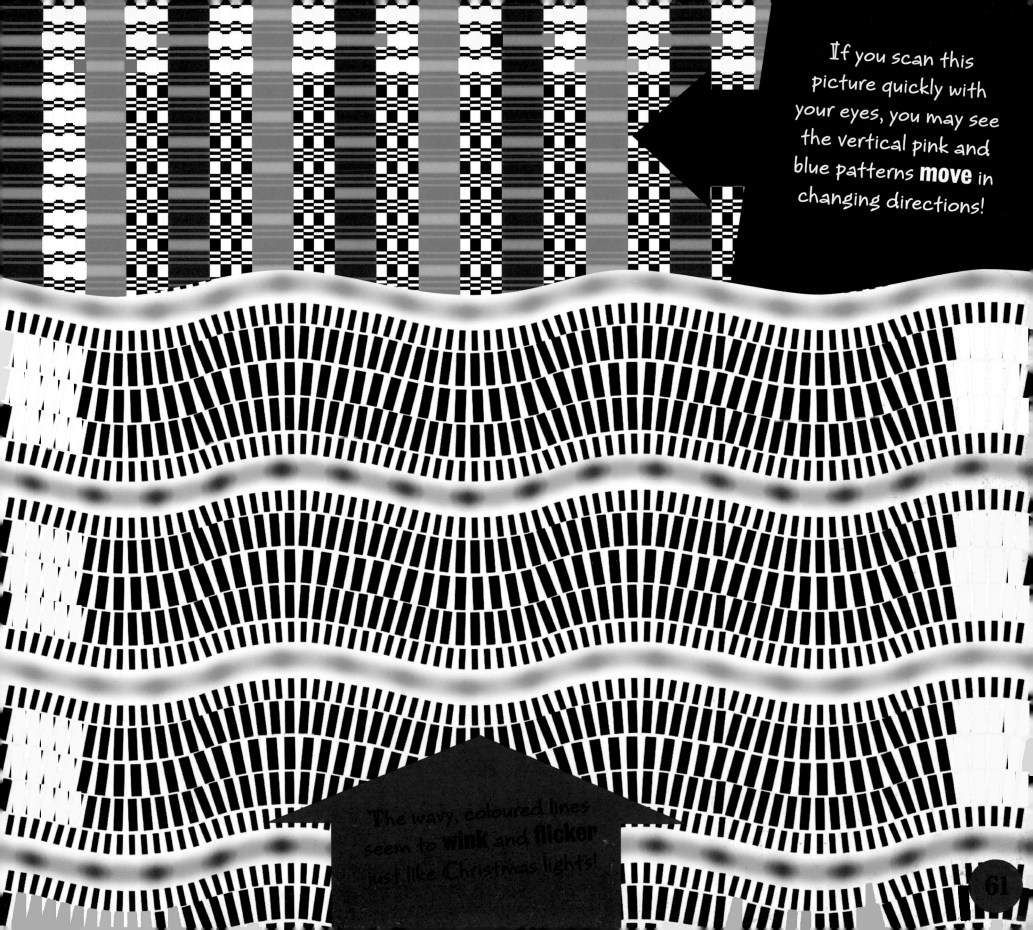

If you scan this picture quickly with your eyes, you may see the vertical pink and blue patterns **move** in changing directions!

The wavy, coloured lines seem to **wink** and **flicker** just like Christmas lights!

61

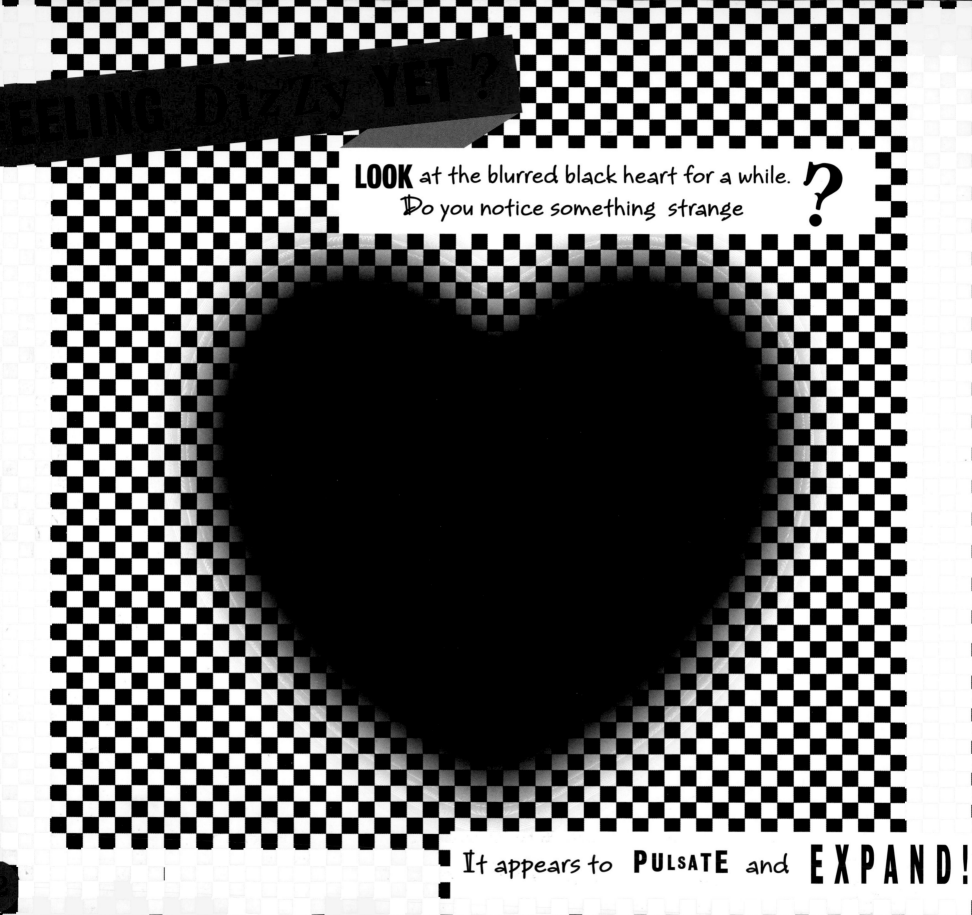

FEELING DIZZY YET?

LOOK at the blurred black heart for a while. Do you notice something strange **?**

It appears to **PULSATE** and **EXPAND!**

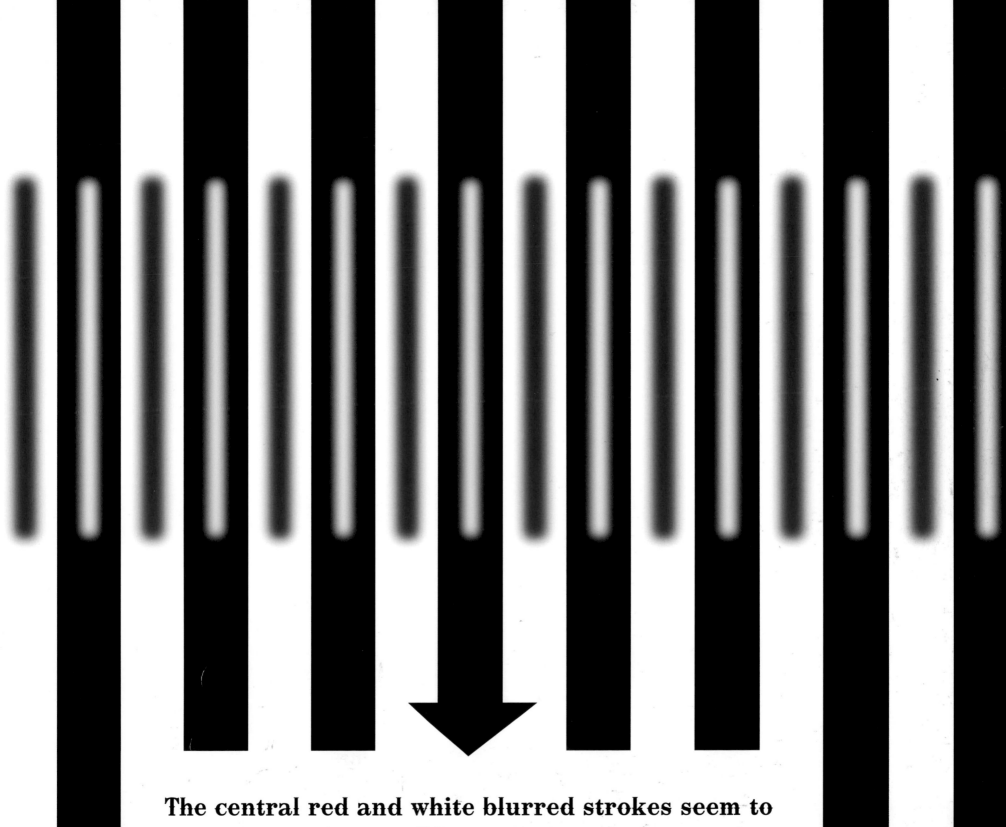

The central red and white blurred strokes seem to
m**o**ve and to **SHRI**nk or **E X P A N D** .

Although this image is of course totally still, the **COFFEE BEANS** seem to J U M P !

Sometimes this illusion works better when you don't look directly at the coffee beans... for example when you are reading this text!

WHAT DO YOU SEE?

Move your head **BACKWARDS** and **FORWARDS**, keeping your eyes fixed on the central cross in the image.

The three circular patterns will start to turn! Your brain is misreading the blurred dots as motion signals - and "thinks" they are actually moving.

Shift your gaze around this pattern and dark dots will appear and disappear at the corners of the white squares.

CAN YOU TELL WHO

IS IN THIS PICTURE?

It's **FRANK... ENSTEIN'S** monster! Look at the image from a distance to see him more clearly.

THIS CIRCULAR SHAPE IS **A MANDALA.**

It pulsates in tune with your brain waves!
Appealing shapes and colour can affect the

67

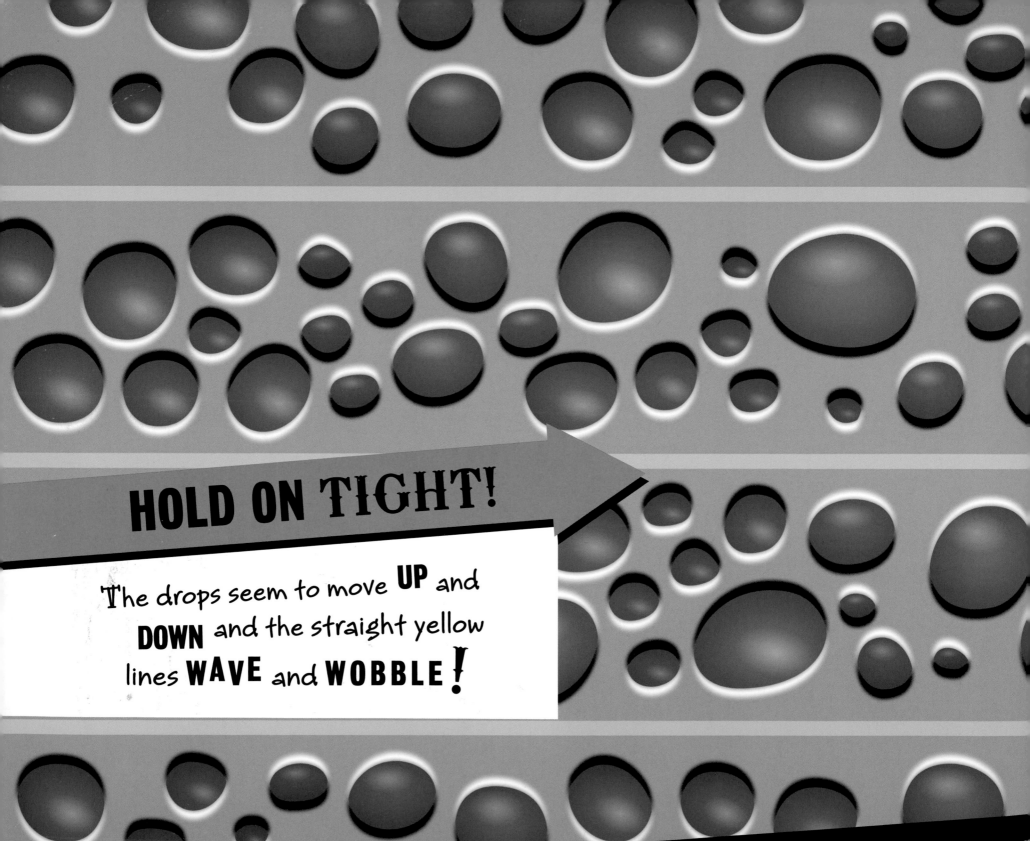

HOLD ON TIGHT!

The drops seem to move **UP** and **DOWN** and the straight yellow lines **WAVE** and **WOBBLE**!

Did you know? An **ILLUSION** of seeing movement triggers similar brain areas as **REAL** motion.

This bat seems to **FLUTTER, MOVE** AND **EXPAND.**

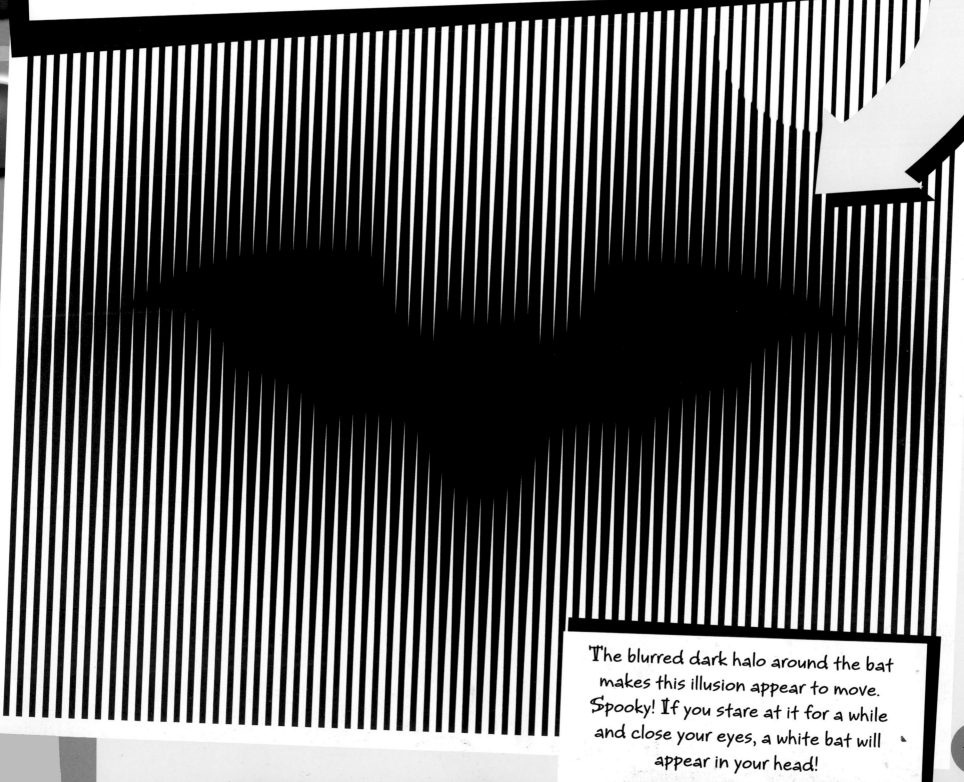

The blurred dark halo around the bat makes this illusion appear to move. Spooky! If you stare at it for a while and close your eyes, a white bat will appear in your head!

IMPOSSIBLE
PUZZLING
CAMOUFLAGED
UNBELIEVABLE
THINGS!

When the lines of a drawing are badly linked, the result can be an "impossible figure": a shape that looks normal at first, but cannot exist in reality.

Depending on the way you look at them, some pictures can also have two different meanings or even hide another picture.

IMPOSSIBLE AQUEDUCT

No builder could construct this!

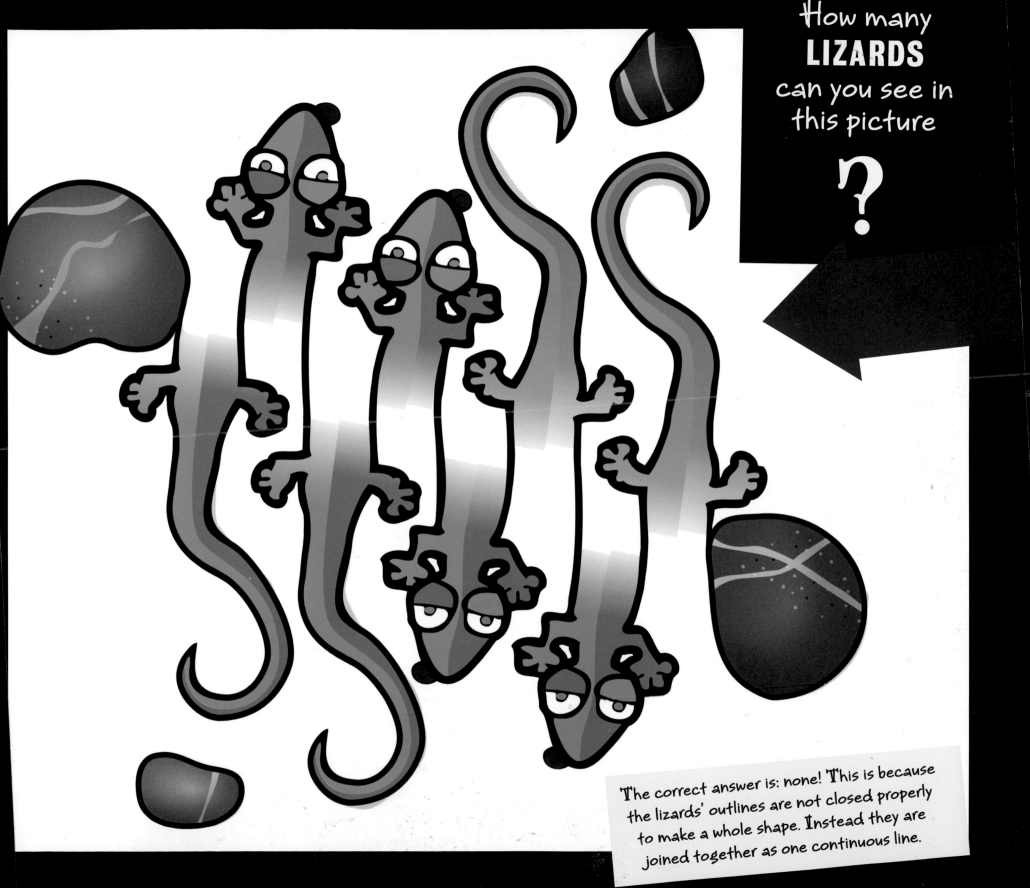

The correct answer is: none! This is because the lizards' outlines are not closed properly to make a whole shape. Instead they are joined together as one continuous line.

CAN YOU SPOT
a COMPLETE FIGURE in this picture?

?

Didn't think so! The top and bottom half of each character aren't actually connected to make a full shape. In fact, each figure is reversed along an axis in the middle of the image, where the green and black shapes are swapped. Can you see where?

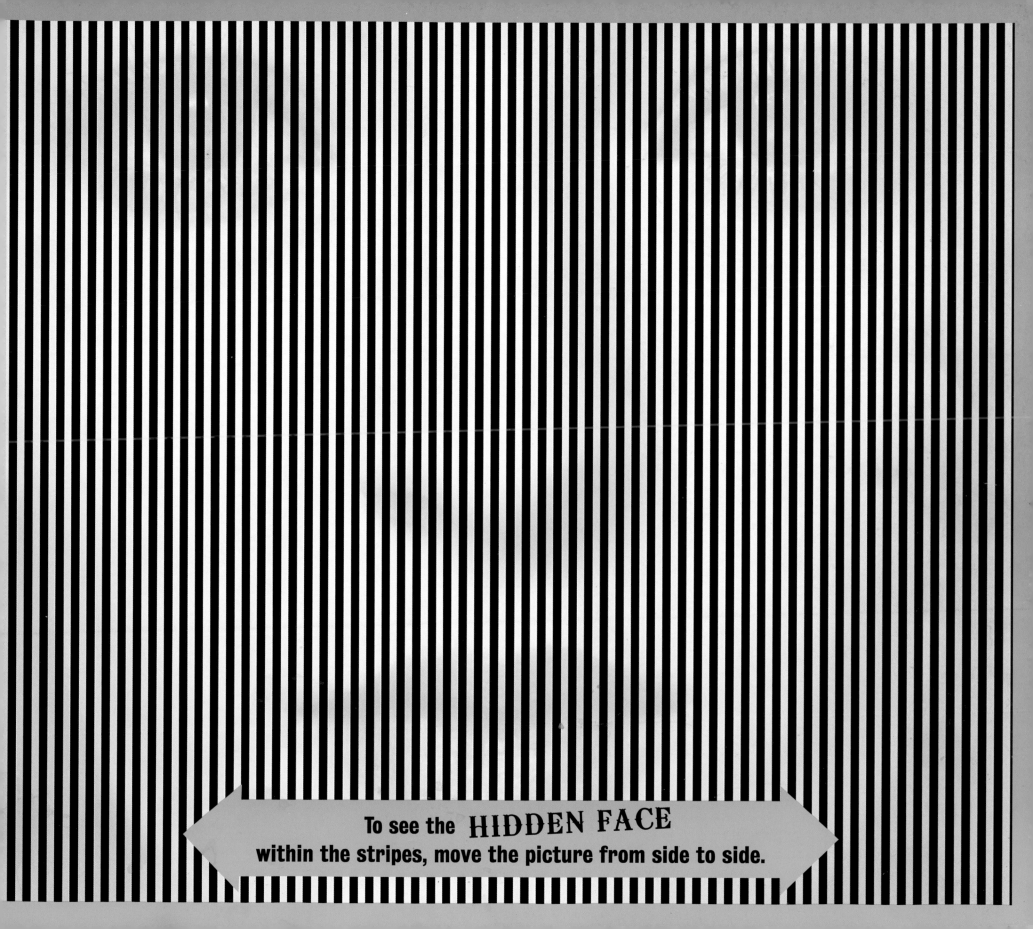

To see the HIDDEN FACE
within the stripes, move the picture from side to side.

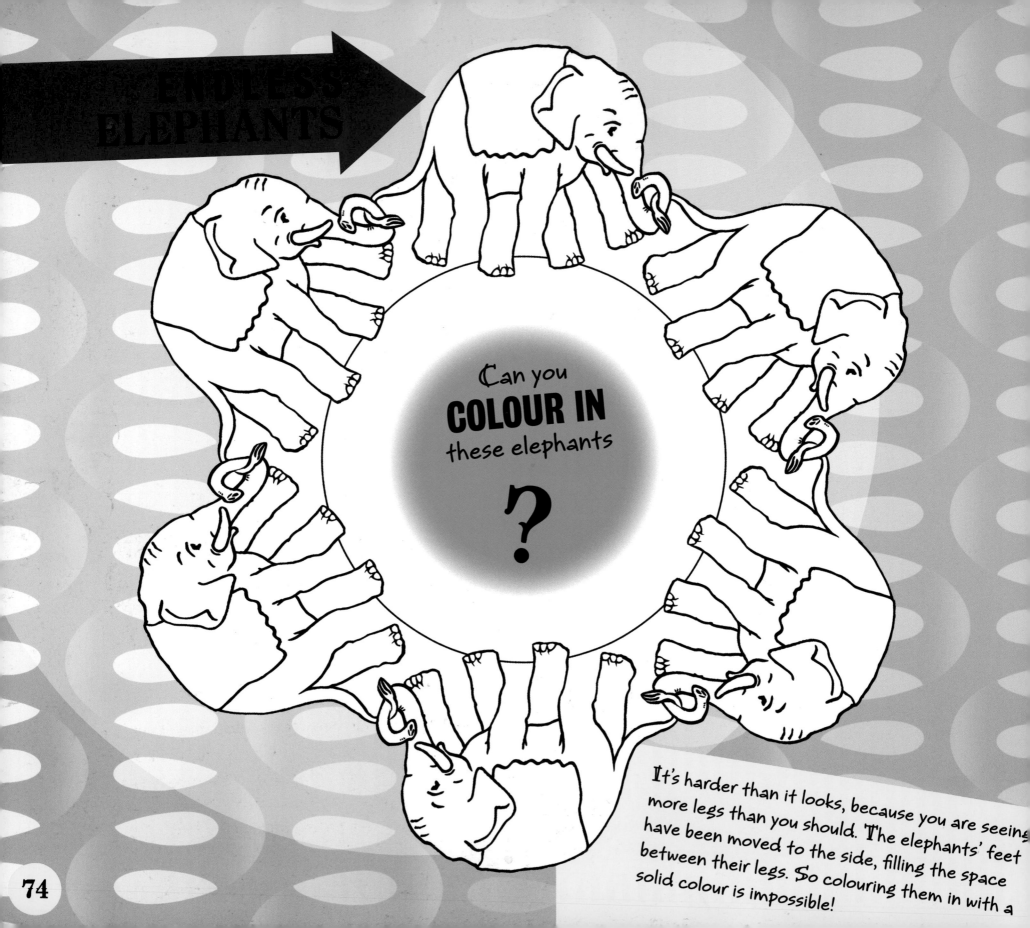

Can you **COLOUR IN** these elephants **?**

It's harder than it looks, because you are seeing more legs than you should. The elephants' feet have been moved to the side, filling the space between their legs. So colouring them in with a solid colour is impossible!

74

Does the window open **outwards** or **inwards?**

?

Is the front door of Lea's house **narrow** or **wide?**

There's no right answer to those questions, because this picture contains "impossible objects". The second marble column of the door blends with the empty space under the arch, and the window faces either to the right or to the left, depending on how you look at it.

If you **LOOK** at the **CENTRE** of this photograph for a while ...

a **SPOOKY FACE** will suddenly **APPEAR** **!**

(Its nose is the woman's shadow.)

This kind of illusion happens because humans have a tendency to see familiar shapes - even if they're not there.

A bar of chocolate is cut into six pieces and put back together to produce an extra piece of chocolate from nothing!

START

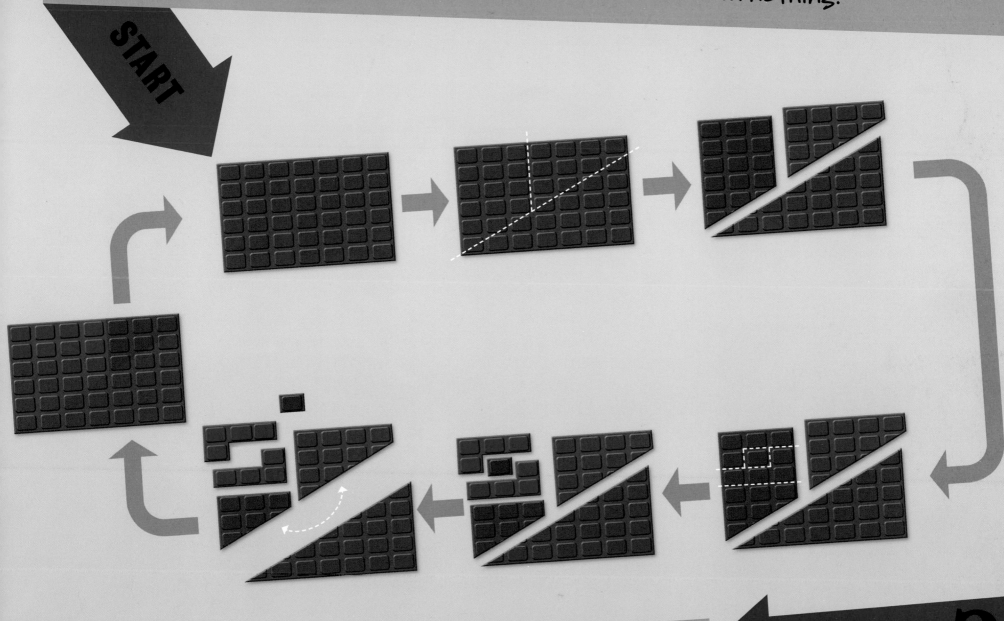

When a small piece of chocolate is removed from the bar and the remaining pieces put back together, they form a slightly shorter rectangle. The difference is too small to see with the naked eye so that the bar looks as if it is the same size as before.

HOW IS THIS POSSIBLE?

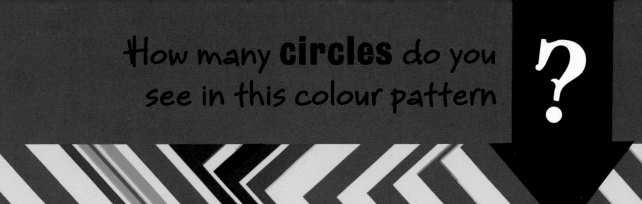

First-time viewers do not usually see the two circles against the colourful background.

WHAT HAPPENS if the girl climbs up the stairs to the platform **?**

The answer is, not much! The platform and stairs form an impossible continuous loop. The girl could walk around in a circle forever and never get any higher!

SIZE AND SHAPE CONFUSION. STRAIGHT or NOT?

The actual size of an object and the size it appears to be are two very different things. Shape confusion and errors in judging size have various causes, including the fact that we think in 3D, even when we look at 2D photos or drawings.

Which goldfish is **longer**?

Both are the same size. The bottom fish seems larger because it is surrounded by a smaller space.

Move your eyes up and down the picture ...

Are the thin, blue lines **straight** and **parallel** to each other?

Although they seem to move away from and get closer to each other, the lines are perfectly parallel! The pattern of leaves in the background creates the illusion that the blue lines are tilting.

This **SNAIL SHELL** looks like a **SPIRAL**, but the recurring pattern is actually made up of several circles!

If you don't believe it, use your finger to trace along the lines.

In these three atoms, the red cores are different sizes.

Which one is the
LARGEST

AND

which one is the
SMALLEST

?

1.

2.

3.

The red disc in figure 1 is the largest, while the disc in figure 3 is the smallest. It's hard to guess the real size of objects, because the perception of size is "relative". That means you judge the size of an object according to the objects around it.

STRAIGHT OR NOT?

?

The chequered frames are perfectly straight! The small black and white squares form wavy lines that interfere with how you see the straight lines, making the frames appear wonky.

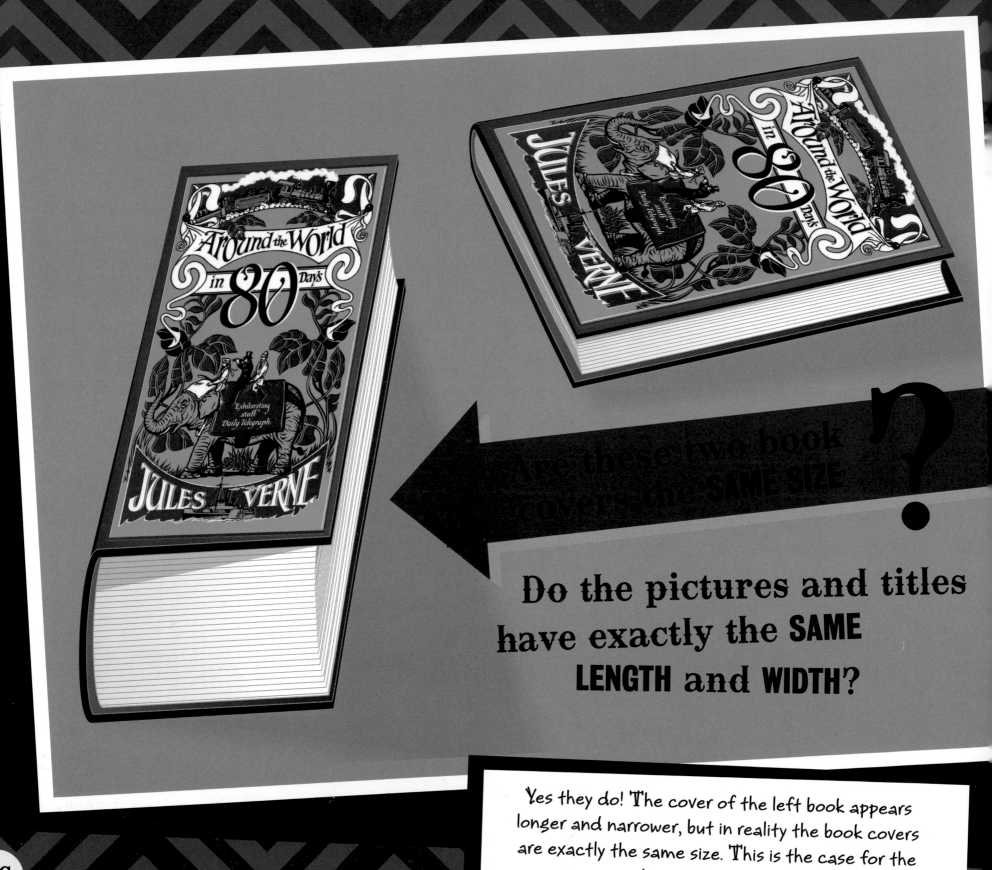

Are these two book covers the SAME SIZE?

Do the pictures and titles have exactly the SAME LENGTH and WIDTH?

Yes they do! The cover of the left book appears longer and narrower, but in reality the book covers are exactly the same size. This is the case for the words and illustrations too!

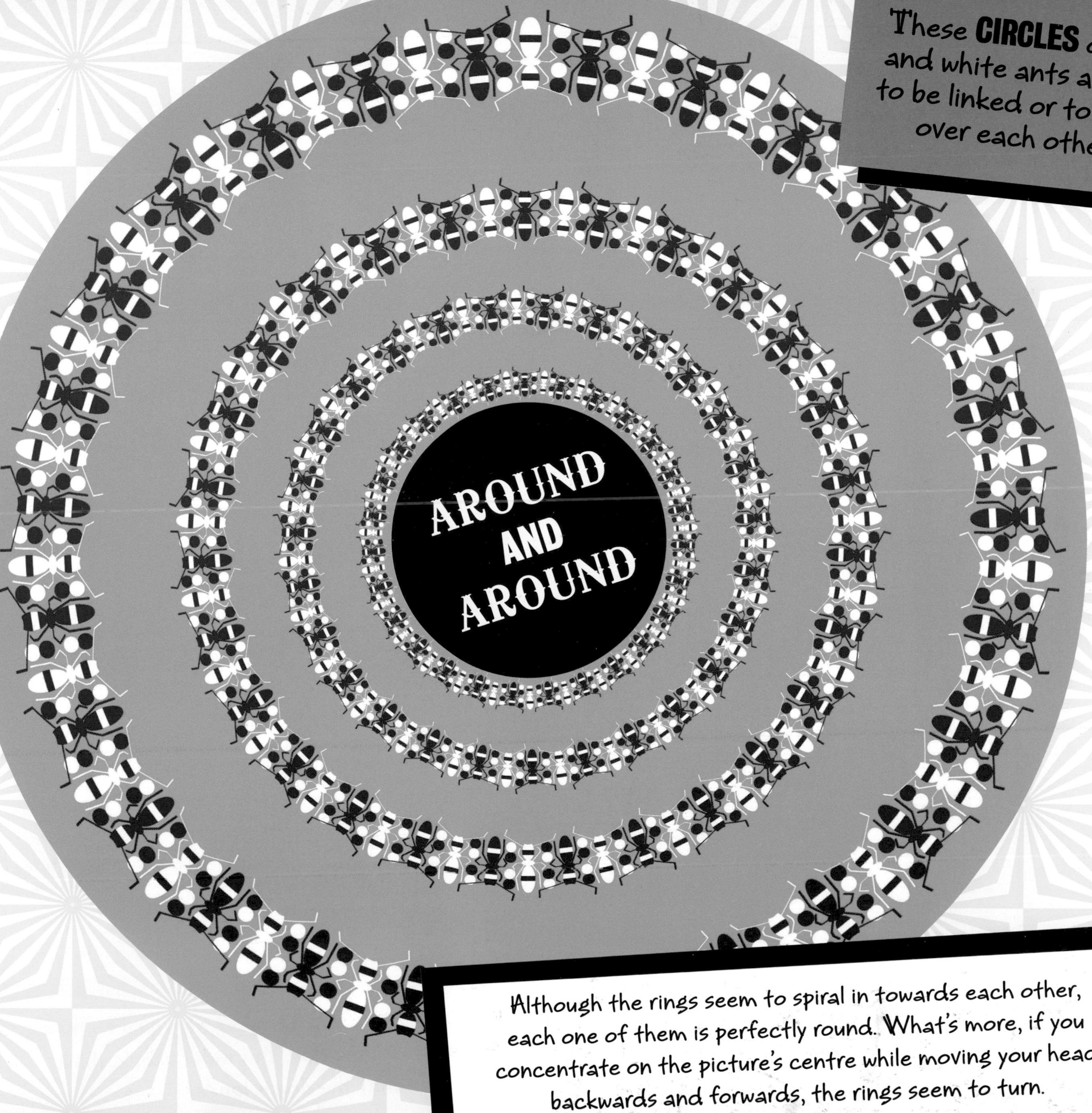

AROUND
AND
AROUND

Although the rings seem to spiral in towards each other, each one of them is perfectly round. What's more, if you concentrate on the picture's centre while moving your head backwards and forwards, the rings seem to turn.

Is the giraffe **TALLER** than the length of the dog ...

OR

is the dog **LONGER** than the height of the giraffe ?

The height of the giraffe is exactly equal to the whole length of the dog. But most people think that the dog is longer.

If you connected the small white spots in the four **RED BALLS** together, would you get a perfect square? What about the spots in the **BLUE BALLS** ?

If you connect the white spots of the blue balls, you will outline a perfect square. You won't in the red.

Look at this dazzling shape!
Can you see its
CURVED SIDES?

It looks as if each side of the shape is on a different level. Follow the rows of black lines and you will see that the whole image is on the same level. The way the lines have been drawn gives you the impression that the sides of the shape are curved.

These green shapes seem to wiggle up and down the page... but if you put a ruler across them, you'll see they form a perfect grid.

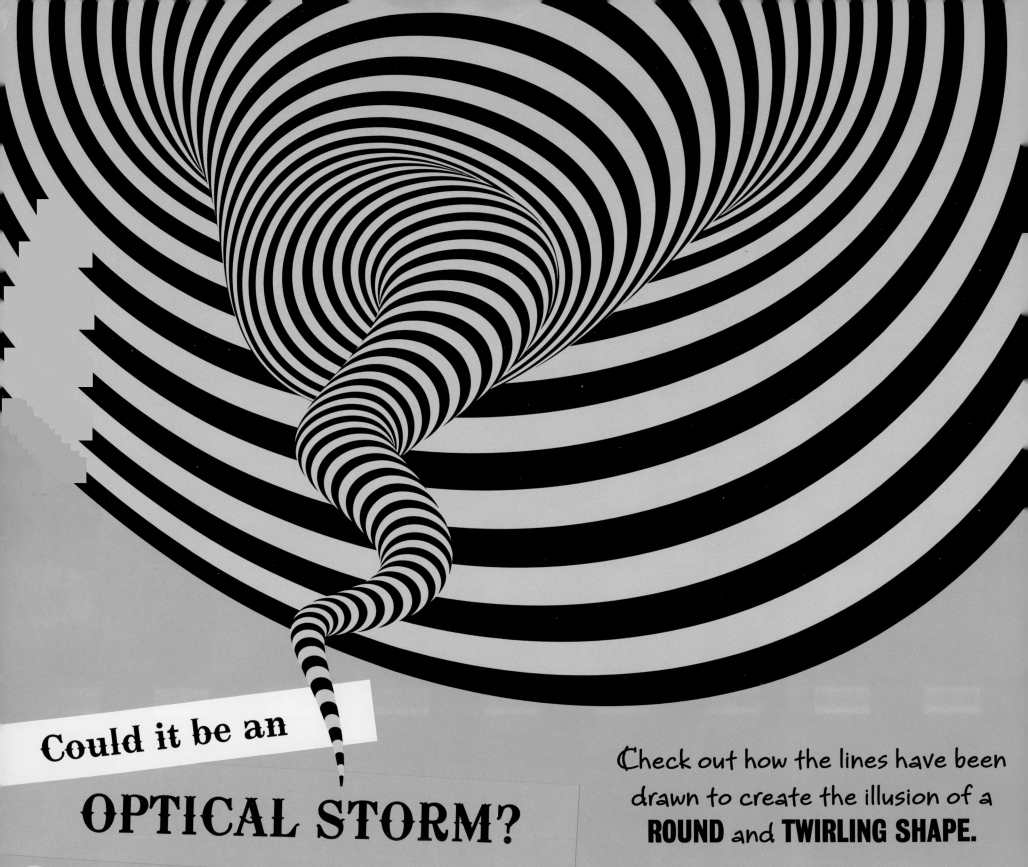

Could it be an

OPTICAL STORM?

Check out how the lines have been drawn to create the illusion of a **ROUND** and **TWIRLING SHAPE.**

Are you feeling **DIZZY?**

THIS IS A CARLTON BOOK

Executive Editors – Selina Wood, Barry Timms, Stephanie Stahl, Joff Brown
Art Editors – Dani Lurie, Emily Clarke
Senior Editor – Anna Bowles
Designer – Rachel Lawston, Ceri Woods
Consultant – Steve Parker
Production – Nicola Davey

Pages 1-47, 90, 92–96 from original book entitled Awesome Optical
Illusions, Artworks and Text © Carlton Books Limited 2012, 2018

Pages 48–89 from original book entitled Super Optical Illusions, Artworks
and Text © Gianni A. Sarcone, giannisarcone.com 2014, 2018

Awesome Optical Illusions first published in 2013 and Super Optical
Illusions first published in 2014 by Carlton Books Limited, an imprint of the
Carlton Publishing Group, 20 Mortimer Street, London W1T 3JW.
This bind-up edition published in 2018.

A catalogue record for this book is available from the British Library.

ISBN: 978-1-78739-163-5

Printed in Dongguan, China

The publishers would like to thank the following sources for their kind permission to reproduce the pictures in this book.

Alamy: /Paul Fleet: 27, 43, 44
Bridgeman Images: /Philip Mould Ltd, London: 26
Getty Images: 39, /Barcroft Media: 28, /Gianni Dagli Orti: 19, /Rian Hughes: 12, /John Lund: 41, /Mike Theiss: 31
iStockphoto: 22, 25, 36, 37
Photos 12: /Oronoz: 29
Gianni A Sarcone, giannisarcone.com: 48–89
Science Photo Library: 13
Shutterstock: /Leo Brazil: 93, /Chris the Composer: 91, /Login: 92, /Olegganko: 2, 90
Thinkstock: 17,
Rebecca Wright: 23, 24, 45, 46, 47

Every effort has been made to acknowledge correctly and contact the source and/or copyright holder of each picture and Carlton Books Limited apologises for any unintentional errors or omissions, which will be corrected in future editions of this book.

The artist and visual researcher Gianni A. Sarcone is the creator and the copyright holder of the pictures and photographs on pages 48–89 re-used from the original book entitled *Super Optical Illusions*.